SAY THIS, NOT THAT

Gentle Parenting Scripts for Your
Teen or Young Adult

Lara Pitocchi

Copyright © 2023 LARAstudio, LLC

All rights reserved

The characters and events portrayed in this book are fictitious. Any similarity to real persons, living or dead, is coincidental and not intended by the author.

No part of this book may be reproduced, or stored in a retrieval system, or transmitted in any form or by any means, electronic, mechanical, photocopying, recording, or otherwise, without express written permission of the publisher.

Cover design by: Art Painter
Library of Congress Control Number: 2018675309
Printed in the United States of America

*To My Shmoopy, whom I love infinity more.
To Keith, whom I listen to, and who listens to me.
To My Misty, whose unconditional love and support has buoyed me throughout my life.
And to Mom and Dad, whom I can call whenever I get out too far over my skis.*

CONTENTS

Title Page	
Copyright	
Dedication	
Introduction	1
Contrasting Parenting Styles	4
How to Use This Book	6
Part 1 - Emotional Turbulence	8
Part 2 - Communication and Connection	13
Part 3 - Social Challenges	18
Part 4 - Health and Wellness	25
Part 5 - Digital World	32
Part 6 - Life Skills	37
Part 7 - Future Planning	42
Part 8 - Risky Encounters	46
Part 9 - Understanding Their World	50
Part 10 - Education	56
A Final Note on Your Empowered Gentle Parenting Journey	69
Your Next Steps to Continue this Empowered Gentle Parenting Journey	71
About The Author	73

INTRODUCTION

Alright, here we go! Buckle up, my parenting friend, because we're embarking on a grand parenting adventure with "Say This Not That: Scripts for the Empowered Gentle Parent of Teens and Young Adults"!

Now, I bet you're clutching this book with both a sense of anticipation and a dash of desperation. Oh, how I can relate! Remember that time I was facing a hurricane in the shape of my three-year-old throwing tantrums? The countless moments I felt like a failure, seething with frustration, on the verge of waving that white flag? You're not alone. We've all been there!

So, before we plunge headlong into this journey, let's chat about parenting styles. These are like the weather systems that shape the climate of our homes. There are four well-known ones - Permissive, Authoritarian, Uninvolved, and Authoritative. Each has its own unique pattern, with a specific blend of warmth and control.

Now, let's talk about the pros and cons of each. You might think permissive parenting - with its warmth and lack of discipline - could be the way to go. Or maybe you're leaning towards the stern but safe harbor of authoritarian parenting? And while being uninvolved might seem like the path of least resistance, it's not the most nurturing. Among all these styles, the real shining star, according to a growing body of research, is the authoritative style.

You see, studies have consistently shown that authoritative parenting is the golden ticket to positive child outcomes. For instance, a study by Padilla-Walker and colleagues in 2016 found that authoritative parenting was associated with positive academic, psychosocial, and behavioral outcomes in children. They posited that this positive effect could be attributed to the balance of responsiveness and demandingness characterizing the authoritative style.

In 2018, a meta-analysis conducted by Pinquart confirmed these findings, linking authoritative parenting to lower levels of problem behavior and higher levels of competencies in children and adolescents.

Furthermore, recent research has extended the benefits of authoritative parenting to digital contexts as well. In a 2020 study, Symons et al. found that teens whose parents engaged in authoritative parenting were less likely to be victimized online. They were also less likely to participate in risky online behaviors.

Now, doesn't that sound like what we all want for our children?

But, wait a minute! What if I told you there's a way to upgrade authoritative parenting to another level? Enter stage right: Gentle Parenting!

Gentle parenting, a sort of authoritative parenting's empathic twin, takes all the goodies - clear boundaries, respect, and guidance - and infuses them with empathy, respect, understanding, and connection. Now, this isn't some new-age, airy-fairy concept. It's backed by science, my friend! Research such as that conducted by Gottman et al., (1997) demonstrates the powerful impact of emotion coaching (a key component of gentle parenting) on children's emotional intelligence and resilience.

Gentle parenting works wonders with all age groups, but it truly shines when dealing with teens and young adults. You know those years when our kiddos seem to morph overnight into these mysterious, volatile beings? Gentle parenting gives us the tools to navigate these turbulent waters with grace and connection.

Now, here's the thing. This book, as comprehensive and transformative as it is, won't create a sustainable change unless you're willing to dig deep. And by digging deep, I mean addressing any underlying generational or other traumas that you might be carrying. Remember, the most empowering changes happen when we're brave enough to face our shadows and heal. And, if you ever need a hand in this challenging but rewarding process, reach out to me at Empowered Gentle Parenting. We're in this together, always.

So, my dear parenting friend, are you ready to embark on this incredible, life-changing journey? To learn how to parent with empathy, respect, and love? To transform your family dynamics? If so, let's dive in head-first! The adventure of gentle parenting awaits!

CONTRASTING PARENTING STYLES

Let's imagine a scenario where a parent is trying to get their teenager, Sam, out of bed to clean up their room. Here's how it could play out in the four recognized parenting styles:

1. Authoritarian: "Sam, get out of bed right now! This room is a mess, it's disgusting. I expect it spotless by lunchtime. No discussion, no excuses. You should be ashamed of living like this."

2. Permissive: "Hey Sam, it would be really nice if you could tidy up your room today, but if you don't want to, that's okay too. Do it whenever you feel like."

3. Neglectful: (Doesn't mention the state of Sam's room or remind him to clean it, despite it being disorganized and dirty.)

4. Authoritative: "Sam, it's time to wake up. You have some responsibilities today. Your room needs to be tidied. It's important to keep our living spaces clean for hygiene and organization. I expect it to be cleaned up before dinner. Let's discuss a plan on how you'll tackle this."

    4a. Gentle Parenting (a type of Authoritative): "Good morning, Sam! I hope you had a good rest. I noticed your room's looking a bit cluttered. How about we create a plan together to clean it up today? Having a clean space could help you find things easier and feel more relaxed. I'm here to help if you need it. How does that sound?"

The gentle parenting approach respects Sam's feelings and autonomy, while still clearly communicating the parent's expectations and the reasoning behind them. It also offers support, enhancing the connection between the parent and the child.

HOW TO USE THIS BOOK

Alright, let's dive into it, dear parenting friend! "Say This Not That: Scripts for the Empowered Gentle Parent of Teens and Young Adults" is crafted to be your trusty companion on your parenting journey.

Here's how to make the most of it:

1. **Familiarize Yourself**: Start by flipping through the pages, getting to know the sections, and soaking in the overall layout of the book. Each part is designed to be both comprehensive and straightforward, presenting an array of scenarios and responses that you may encounter in your parenting journey.
2. **Find Your Need**: This book works best when it's catering to your specific needs. Is your teenager pushing boundaries? Or perhaps your young adult is struggling with independence? Identify the scenarios most relevant to you and head straight to those sections.
3. **Try It On**: This isn't a book about radical overnight change; it's about trying on gentle parenting for size. Pick a script or two that resonate with your current parenting situation. Incorporate these responses into your everyday interactions with your child. Observe the changes, in both your child and yourself.
4. **Be Patient**: Remember, the change isn't instant. Parenting, like life, is a marathon, not a sprint. Gentle parenting isn't about a quick fix; it's about creating a lasting, positive change in the way you relate to your

child. Give the process time, and extend the same patience to yourself that you're learning to give your child.
5. **Reflect and Revise**: The beauty of this approach is in its flexibility. If a script isn't landing quite right, don't worry. Use it as a springboard to adapt your own response that maintains the core principles of gentle parenting: respect, understanding, and nurturing autonomy.
6. **Stay Open**: As you delve deeper into the gentle parenting approach, you may be surprised to find yourself questioning some long-held beliefs or facing some of your own past traumas. This is part of the process, and it's okay.

Remember, this book is not intended to be a panacea for all parenting challenges. It's an invitation to explore a new way of interacting with your teens and young adults—one that emphasizes empathy, respect, and communication. Your new mantra? Be loving, fair, and firm. So go ahead and give gentle parenting a try.

This could be the first step in a transformation not only in your parenting style, but also in your relationship with your child. Welcome to your empowered gentle parenting journey!

PART 1 - EMOTIONAL TURBULENCE

Ah, emotional turbulence. It's like living with a mini roller coaster that's discovered Red Bull. We've all been there, and if you're reading this guide, I'm guessing you're in the thick of it right now. This section is all about helping you ride those ups and downs like a pro-surfer on a gnarly wave.

First things first, let's establish why this calls for a gentle parenting touch. Traditional parenting methods, where authority is not to be challenged, often stifle emotional expression and discourage open dialogue about feelings. The unintended consequence? A child who feels misunderstood, invalidated, or unheard. With gentle parenting, however, we create an atmosphere of understanding and validation where emotions aren't just dismissed as teen drama but recognized as real, important experiences.

Here's the game-changer. The long-term payoff of this style of parenting isn't just fewer slammed doors and less sulking (although those are a nice bonus!). By validating and working through these turbulent emotions, we deepen the connection with our child, paving the way for an enduring relationship based on respect and mutual understanding.

But let's remember, we're all delightfully human. Some days will be messier than others, and not every conversation will end with a heartfelt hug and a sharing of the deepest feelings. That's okay. It's not about getting it right every time, but about committing to try again, always striving for connection and understanding.

Gone awry before? Welcome to the club. Repairing is as important, if not more, than getting it right the first time. Apologize, acknowledge your mistakes, and assure them of your commitment to do better. It's not about sweeping things under the rug but cleaning up together, reinforcing the bond through honesty and humility.

So, let's dive in. The turbulence may be wild, but the destination – a lasting, loving relationship – is well worth the ride.

1.1. Navigating Emotional Outbursts

Emotional outbursts are tough for everyone involved. Here are some empathetic responses:

1. **Say This:** "I can see you're really upset about this. Let's talk it through when you're ready."
Not That: "Stop overreacting!"

2. **Say This:** "I see that you're angry. I'm here for you when you're ready to talk calmly."
Not That: "Don't yell at me!"

3. **Say This:** "Your feelings are important. Can we try to discuss this in a calm manner?"
Not That: "You're being ridiculous!"

4. **Say This:** "I understand you're upset. I'd like us to communicate respectfully."
Not That: "Don't talk to me like that!"

5. **Say This:** "If you need some space, that's okay. We can talk when you're feeling calmer."
Not That: "You can't storm out every time!"

6. **Say This:** "I see you're really frustrated. Can we take some deep breaths together?"
Not That: "Stop yelling right now!"

7. **Say This:** "You seem really upset, would you like to talk about it?"
Not That: "There's no reason to be this upset!"

8. **Say This:** "I'm here for you, let's figure out what you can do when you're feeling this way."
Not That: "You need to control yourself!"

9. **Say This:** "It's okay to feel angry, but we need to find a safe way to express it."
Not That: "Don't be disrespectful!"

10. **Say This:** "These feelings are tough, but they will pass. I'm right here with you."
Not That: "You're being overly dramatic."

1.2. Self-Esteem

Nurturing your teen's self-esteem is crucial. Here's how to offer support:

1. **Say This:** "You're uniquely you, and that's what makes you special."

Not That: "Why can't you be more like (insert comparison)?"

2. **Say This:** "I believe in you, even when you find it hard to believe in yourself."

Not That: "Stop doubting yourself."

3. **Say This:** "I understand it's a big deal for you, and I'm here to support you."

Not That: "It's not a big deal."

4. **Say This:** "I see that you're worried. Let's talk about it."

Not That: "What's there to worry about?"

5. **Say This:** "I know it's hard sometimes, but remember, it's okay to be you."

Not That: "Just be confident."

1.3. Body Image

Promote positive body image with these responses:

1. **Say This:** "You're perfect the way you are, and it's important to be healthy."

Not That: "Maybe you should diet/exercise."

2. **Say This:** "Let's focus on making choices that make us feel good and strong."

Not That: "You don't need to eat that."

3. **Say This:** "It's more important how you feel about yourself. How can I support you?"

Not That: "I think you're perfect."

4. **Say This:** "You're beautiful inside and out, but remember, your self-worth isn't defined by your appearance."
Not That: "Don't worry about your looks."

5. **Say This:** "Change can be hard. I'm here for you every step of the way."
Not That: "Your body will change, don't worry."

PART 2 - COMMUNICATION AND CONNECTION

Well, you've survived the emotional turbulence (for now), so welcome to the next thrilling chapter - communication and connection. This stage feels like trying to tune into a radio station while driving through a tunnel, frustrating and full of static. But fear not! I've got your back.

Now, let's chat about why this stage is prime time for gentle parenting. The authoritarian style, while it might offer short-term obedience, tends to lead to a long-term disconnect. It's like putting a band-aid on a bullet wound - it might stop the bleeding for a moment, but it doesn't solve the root problem. Gentle parenting, on the other hand, treats the wound, encouraging open, respectful conversations which help to foster a deeper understanding.

And this is where the magic happens. The long-term benefits of this communication style go way beyond just having a chat about curfews. It means laying the foundation for a relationship based on mutual respect, understanding, and genuine connection. This isn't just about getting through the teenage years without too many gray hairs; it's about building a lifelong bond.

Of course, we are all gloriously human. This means we'll get it wrong sometimes. There'll be raised voices, heated debates, and even the odd slammed door. And that's okay. We are all learning here. The goal isn't perfection; it's progression. It's about trying to understand and be understood a little better each day.

And if you've taken a wrong turn in the past? Don't worry,

detours are part of the journey. Repairing the relationship isn't about pretending mistakes didn't happen; it's about acknowledging them, apologizing, and making a conscious effort to do better. Because ultimately, we're all in this together, learning as we go.

So, ready to turn down the static and tune into connection? Let's go!

2.1. Communication Gap

Bridging the communication gap is an ongoing process. Here are some suggestions:

1. **Say This:** "I'm really interested in what you're saying. Let's make sure we understand each other."
Not That: "You're not making sense."

2. **Say This:** "It's important for me to understand your viewpoint. Can we talk more about it?"
Not That: "I don't understand what you're talking about."

3. **Say This:** "Can you explain more about this? I want to fully understand you."
Not That: "This conversation is going nowhere."

4. **Say This:** "I may not fully understand yet, but I'm here to listen and learn."
Not That: "You're just not explaining it right."

5. **Say This:** "I appreciate your patience while we navigate this conversation. Let's continue when you're ready."
Not That: "I can't talk to you when you're like this."

2.2 Acting Out

Try these scripts when outbursts (physical or verbal) are a problem:

1. **Say This:** "It seems like you're having a tough time, can we take a break and regroup?"
Not That: "Why can't you just behave?"

2. **Say This:** "I understand you're upset, but hitting is not okay. Let's find another way to express your anger."
Not That: "That's it, you're in time out!"

3. **Say This:** "You're really struggling with listening today. What can we do to make this better?"
Not That: "You never listen!"

4. **Say This:** "You seem to have a lot of energy right now. Would running around outside help?"

Not That: "Stop acting wild!"

5. **Say This:** "Your behavior is telling me you're upset about something. Can we talk about it?"

Not That: "You're being naughty on purpose."

2.2. Disrespectful Attitude

Maintaining respect in tense situations is key. Try these approaches:

1. **Say This:** "I respect you, and I'd like the same from you."

Not That: "Don't disrespect me!"

2. **Say This:** "Let's communicate our thoughts without blaming or insulting each other."

Not That: "You're being rude!"

3. **Say This:** "We can disagree respectfully. Let's try to understand each other."
Not That: "Don't talk back to me!"

4. **Say This:** "Our conversations are more productive when we talk respectfully. Can we try that?"
Not That: "Don't give me that attitude!"

5. **Say This:** "I know we're upset, but we can still respect each other."
Not That: "That's no way to talk to me!"

2.3. Independence

Encourage your teen's journey to independence with these responses:

1. **Say This:** "I trust your judgment. I'm here if you need advice."
Not That: "You're not ready for this."

2. **Say This:** "Let's talk about the pros and cons before you decide."
Not That: "You're making a mistake."

3. **Say This:** "It's your decision, and I support you in making responsible choices."
Not That: "I don't agree with your choice."

4. **Say This:** "Mistakes are part of growing up. You're learning, and I'm here for you."
Not That: "I told you so."

5. **Say This:** "I know you can handle this. Remember, you can always ask for help."
Not That: "You can't do it alone."

PART 3 - SOCIAL CHALLENGES

Okay, parents! We're navigating the hairpin turns of social challenges. Yes, we've all been through this roller coaster ride of peer pressure, first love, and the quest for identity. As if adolescence wasn't tricky enough already, right?

This is where the gentle approach to parenting shifts into high gear. Traditional or authoritarian parenting styles might be tempting when we see our kids standing on the edge of social precipices. It's the parental equivalent of wanting to grab the wheel when a learner driver takes a turn too fast. But remember, our role is to be the navigation system, not the driver.

Overbearing control can lead to rebellion, resentment, or reliance on peer approval over parental advice. Gentle parenting, on the other hand, guides rather than commands. It respects their growing autonomy while providing a safety net of sound advice and unconditional love.

The long-term benefits? Trust me, they're worth it. A gentle approach nurtures resilience, self-confidence, and the ability to make informed choices - skills that will serve them well into adulthood. Plus, it builds a bridge of trust between you and your teen that can weather any storm, be it a break-up or a bad grade.

Hey, we're all human here, and that means we're perfectly imperfect. So, yes, you'll stumble. You'll face some roadblocks, maybe even a detour or two. But remember, every setback is a setup for a comeback. Every mistake is an opportunity to grow.

Had a few bumpy rides in the past? No problem. Fixing a punctured relationship isn't about pretending the hole doesn't exist. It's about patching it up and learning how to avoid those sharp objects in the future. Because in this journey, the only wrong turn is refusing to turn around.

Ready to navigate the thrilling twists and turns of social challenges? Let's hit the road!

3.1 Peer Pressure

Peer pressure can be daunting for teens and young adults. Here's how to offer support:

1. **Say This:** "I understand you want to fit in with your friends, but remember that it's okay to make different

choices if you're uncomfortable with something."
Not That: "You're not hanging out with those kids anymore. They're bad influences."

2. **Say This:** "Saying 'no' can be really tough sometimes. Would it help to role-play some situations?"
Not That: "Just say no! It's not that hard!"

3. **Say This:** "Each person is unique and has their strengths. Let's talk about yours."
Not That: "Why can't you be more like [sibling/friend]?"

4. **Say This:** "It's okay to want to be part of the group. It's also okay to make choices that reflect who you are."
Not That: "You're always following the crowd. Don't you have a mind of your own?"

5. **Say This:** "You have a bright future. Remember, the choices you make now can impact that. Can we talk about some strategies for handling peer pressure?"
Not That: "Are you really going to ruin your future because of them?"

6. **Say This:** "Friends can influence us a lot. It's important to think about if their choices are right for you."
Not That: "If your friends jumped off a bridge, would you?"

7. **Say This:** "I understand you want to fit in, but true friends will like you for you."
Not That: "You shouldn't care what others think."

8. **Say This:** "It's hard when friends want to do things we don't. Let's think of some ways you can handle that."
Not That: "You need to stop being influenced by others."

9. **Say This:** "Your decisions should be based on what you think is right, not what your friends think."
Not That: "You just need to toughen up."

10. **Say This:** "Facing peer pressure is tough, but I believe in your ability to make the right choices."
Not That: "You can't let them walk all over you."

3.2 Dating and Relationships

Dating and relationships bring a new set of challenges for teens and young adults. Here's how you can foster open communication and respect:

1. **Say This:** "I understand you might be feeling a lot of emotions being in a relationship. Let's talk about boundaries and respect."
Not That: "You're too young to be dating."

2. **Say This:** "It's great that you're enjoying your time with your partner. Remember, though, the importance of balance in relationships."
Not That: "You're always with your boyfriend/girlfriend. Don't you have any other friends?"

3. **Say This:** "I worry about your feelings, as relationships can sometimes lead to hurt. Let's talk about the signs of a healthy relationship."
Not That: "I don't want you to get hurt."

4. **Say This:** "I notice this relationship seems to be causing

3. **Say This:** "The effort you've put into this project is commendable, irrespective of the grade."
Not That: "Why isn't this an A?"

4. **Say This:** "Remember, school is about more than just grades."
Not That: "You need to focus more on your report card."

5. **Say This:** "Mistakes are a part of learning. Let's see what this one can teach us."
Not That: "How can you keep getting this wrong?"

6. **Say This:** "Let's brainstorm some ways to help you stay organized with your assignments."
Not That: "Your lack of organization is frustrating."

7. **Say This:** "I've noticed you're having some issues with your classmates. Can we talk about it?"
Not That: "Just ignore them."

8. **Say This:** "Let's figure out a study schedule that fits your needs."
Not That: "You always leave everything until the last minute."

9. **Say This:** "It's okay to seek help from your teacher. They're there to guide you."
Not That: "Figure it out yourself."

10. **Say This:** "Balancing academics and extracurricular activities is key to a well-rounded education."
Not That: "You're spending too much time on non-academic activities."

some tension. Would you like to talk about it?"
Not That: "This relationship is causing too much drama."

5. **Say This:** "You deserve respect in all relationships. Do you feel respected and valued in this one?"
Not That: "I don't like the way they're treating you."

6. **Say This:** "I'm here to support you, even in tough relationship moments."
Not That: "I told you they weren't right for you."

7. **Say This:** "Love should always be respectful. How are you feeling in your relationship?"
Not That: "You shouldn't let them treat you like that."

8. **Say This:** "You're deserving of a relationship that brings you joy."
Not That: "You can do better than them."

9. **Say This:** "It's normal to feel a range of emotions in a relationship. Let's talk about it."
Not That: "Relationships are supposed to make you happy."

10. **Say This:** "If you're ever uncomfortable in your relationship, remember it's okay to seek help."
Not That: "You should just break up with them."

3.3 Identity and Self-expression

Identity and self-expression are important facets of a teen's or young adult's life. Here's how you can provide support and acceptance:

1. **Say This:** "Your style is unique to you. How does expressing yourself in this way make you feel?"

   Not That: "Why can't you dress/behave like other kids?"

2. **Say This:** "It's okay to explore different parts of who you are. How can I best support you during this time?"

   Not That: "You're just going through a phase."

3. **Say This:** "I may not fully understand your choices, but I respect your right to express yourself. Can you help me understand better?"

   Not That: "I don't understand why you're doing this."

4. **Say This:** "It's great that you're confident enough to be different. Let's talk about the importance of staying true to yourself."

   Not That: "Why are you always trying to stand out?"

5. **Say This:** "My goal has always been to raise you to be a confident and kind individual. Let's talk about how your current choices align with those values."

   Not That: "I didn't raise you to be like this."

6. **Say This:** "Your identity is yours to define. I support you exploring who you are."
Not That: "Why can't you be like everyone else?"

7. **Say This:** "It's brave to be yourself when everyone else is trying to fit in."
Not That: "You're just going through a phase."

8. **Say This**: "Your unique qualities make you the wonderful person you are."
Not That: "Why would you want to express yourself that way?"

9. **Say This:** "Everyone has their own path. I'm proud of you for finding yours."
Not That: "This isn't the life I imagined for you."

10. **Say This:** "I'm learning from your journey, too. Let's grow together."
Not That: "I don't understand why you're doing this."

PART 4 - HEALTH AND WELLNESS

Health and wellness! It's like trying to find a unicorn in a field of horses. Just when you think you've spotted it - bam - it morphs back into a pony. The challenge of maintaining good mental and physical health is a tricky one, and it becomes a whole new ball game when you're parenting teens and young adults.

If we take an authoritarian approach to this topic, it might look something like us imposing stringent rules about diet, exercise, and even mental health without taking their feelings and viewpoints into account. And we all know how that usually ends - with rebellion, secrecy, and possibly some sneaky junk food eating behind our backs.

The magic of gentle parenting is that it flips the narrative. We become their partners, not dictators, in the journey towards good health. We show empathy for their struggles, help them build resilience, and above all, remind them that it's perfectly okay not to be okay sometimes. The potential payoff is massive - we're helping them create habits and mindsets that can positively impact their health throughout their lives.

We're all human here, and it's crucial to remember that slip-ups will happen. There will be days when the lure of a deep-dish pizza will overpower the best of intentions or when they'll confide in us about the heaviness clouding their minds. It's not about reacting perfectly but responding with compassion and understanding.

Maybe you've previously resorted to laying down the law about health-related matters, and it hasn't gone well. The beauty of this relationship is that it's never too late to repair it. Admit where you've gone wrong, open up a dialogue about how you can better support them, and most importantly, be patient.

So, let's explore how to help our teens and young adults navigate their health and wellness journey with understanding and respect. It's an ongoing process, but hey, the best things in life usually are!

4.1. Mental Health Concerns

Mental health difficulties are increasingly common. Here's how to approach it:

1. **Say This:** "It's okay to have tough days. Would you like to

talk about what's going on?"
Not That: "You have nothing to be sad about."

2. **Say This:** "Your feelings are important. I'm here to listen."
Not That: "Don't overreact."

3. **Say This:** "Seeking help is a sign of strength. Let's explore options together."
Not That: "Snap out of it."

4. **Say This:** "It's okay to take time for yourself when you're feeling overwhelmed."
Not That: "You're always in your room."

5. **Say This:** "Your mental health matters. Let's prioritize it together."
Not That: "Just be positive."

4.2. Health and Fitness

Here's how to talk about health and fitness without inducing pressure:

1. **Say This:** "Taking care of our bodies is important, but looks aren't everything."
Not That: "You should lose/gain weight."

2. **Say This:** "Physical activity can help us feel better. What activities do you enjoy?"
Not That: "You're always sitting around."

3. **Say This:** "It's about balance, not restriction. Enjoy your favorite foods without guilt."
Not That: "Should you really be eating that?"

4. **Say This:** "Listening to your body is important. Let's learn to do that together."
Not That: "You're always making excuses."

5. **Say This:** "Health is personal. You don't have to compare

yourself to others."
Not That: "Why can't you be more like [insert name]?"

4.3 Body Positivity

Teaching your teen to embrace their body positively is crucial in an image-conscious world. Try these supportive phrases:

1. **Say This**: "Your body is unique and amazing just the way it is."

Not That: "Maybe you should lose a few pounds."

2. **Say This**: "Let's focus on eating healthy because it makes us feel good, not to look a certain way."

Not That: "Are you sure you want to eat that?"

3. **Say This**: "I admire your confidence and the way you carry yourself."

Not That: "Why can't you dress more like your friends?"

4. **Say This**: "Clothes are about expressing yourself. Let's find something that feels true to you."

Not That: "That outfit is not flattering on your body type."

5. **Say This**: "Your body's changes are natural and beautiful. If you have questions, I'm here."

Not That: "You're growing up too fast, and I don't like it."

6. **Say This**: "Comparing ourselves to others can be harmful. What do you love about yourself?"

Not That: "Why can't you look more like this celebrity?"

7. **Say This**: "Media images aren't always real. Your authentic self is what's truly beautiful."

Not That: "If you worked out more, you could look like that."

8. **Say This**: "Your self-love inspires me. Let's keep focusing on what we like about ourselves."

Not That: "Stop being so vain about your appearance."

9. **Say This**: "It's okay to feel how you do about your body, but remember, I think you're perfect."

Not That: "Don't be so sensitive about your appearance."

10. **Say This**: "Other people's comments reflect on them, not you. You're beautiful inside and out."

Not That: "Maybe they're right, you could try to change."

4.4 Understanding Consent

Teaching teens about consent and respecting boundaries is fundamental for healthy relationships. Here are some affirming dialogues to guide these important conversations:

1. **Say This**: "Consent means actively agreeing to something. It's crucial in all relationships."
Not That: "If they didn't say 'no,' it means 'yes.'"

2. **Say This**: "You always have the right to say 'no' at any time, and that should be respected."
Not That: "You said 'yes' before, so you can't change your

mind now."

3. **Say This**: "Let's talk about what consent means and why it's important for everyone involved."
Not That: "It's just common sense; you don't need to talk about it."

4. **Say This**: "Asking for consent is a sign of respect and care in a relationship."
Not That: "Asking for permission ruins the moment."

5. **Say This**: "It's never too late to talk about boundaries and what feels comfortable for you."
Not That: "It's awkward to talk about this now."

6. **Say This**: "Consent is ongoing; it's good to check in with each other regularly."
Not That: "You don't need to keep asking; it ruins the flow."

7. **Say This**: "Your feelings and comfort level are always valid. Let's discuss them openly."
Not That: "Don't be so sensitive; it's not a big deal."

8. **Say This**: "It's okay to have questions about consent, and I'm here to answer them."
Not That: "You should already know this by now."

9. **Say This**: "Respecting someone's 'no' is just as important as hearing a 'yes.'"
Not That: "A 'no' is just a 'yes' waiting to happen."

10. **Say This**: "Everyone's boundaries are different; understanding them makes for healthier connections."
Not That: "If they're okay with it, why aren't you?"

PART 5 - DIGITAL WORLD

Ah, the digital world. The one place where kids seem to know more than their parents. It's like trying to navigate through a bustling city where everyone but you speaks an alien language. What TikTok dance is *that*? And why is everyone obsessed with this 'meme'?

The common authoritarian approach to the digital world often involves strict screen time limits, controlling online activities, and sometimes even complete digital bans. But let's be honest, that's like trying to hold back the tide with a broom. Not only does this lead to secretive online behavior, it also robs them of the chance to develop a healthy digital life.

On the flip side, gentle parenting embraces the digital world and focuses on teaching our teens and young adults how to navigate it responsibly. The benefits? They develop a healthy understanding of the digital landscape, online etiquette, and crucially, learn how to protect themselves online.

We need to remember that even in this digital world, we're all just humans behind screens. And humans, well, we mess up sometimes. So, we'll have moments when we're staring at a screen, dumbfounded by something we just discovered about our teen's online life. But it's all part of the process.

If your past digital parenting style was more watchdog than guide, it's never too late to switch gears. The key lies in openly acknowledging the past and expressing a genuine desire to understand their digital world. The digital age is here to stay, so we might as well get on board.

So let's dive into the digital ocean together. Fear not, gentle parenting is like having a digital life-jacket. It keeps you afloat while you learn to navigate the ebb and flow of the online world. Trust me, it's an adventure worth taking.

5.1. Social Media and Screen Time

With digital technology being ubiquitous, here's how to talk about it:

1. **Say This:** "The digital world can be overwhelming. Let's talk about healthy boundaries."
   Not That: "You're always on your phone."

2. **Say This:** "Social media portrays highlight reels. Remember, everyone has struggles."
Not That: "Stop comparing yourself to people online."

3. **Say This:** "Balancing screen time and offline activities can help us feel better."
Not That: "You're addicted to your phone."

4. **Say This:** "There's more to life than what's on the screen. Let's explore those things."
Not That: "You're missing out on real life."

5. **Say This:** "Privacy and safety online is crucial. Let's discuss how to ensure that."
Not That: "Are you sure you should be sharing that?"

5.2. Cyberbullying

This is an important and sensitive issue. Here's how to tackle it:

1. **Say This:** "If you're ever targeted online, it's not your fault. We can report it and take necessary steps."
Not That: "Ignore it. It's just online."

2. **Say This:** "Kindness matters, both online and offline. Let's foster it."
Not That: "Did you do something to provoke them?"

3. **Say This:** "Your worth isn't determined by what someone says about you online."
Not That: "It's just words."

4. **Say This:** "Let's create a safe online environment together. You can always talk to me about anything."
Not That: "You're too sensitive."

5. **Say This:** "Remember, it's okay to disengage from toxic online spaces."
Not That: "It's all part of being online."

5.3 Cyber Safety

Try these phrases when online habits are a sticking point:

1. **Say This:** "Online friends can be fun, but remember we don't share personal details with people we haven't met in person."

   Not That: "You shouldn't be making friends online."

2. **Say This:** "Not everything on the internet is true or reliable. Let's learn how to evaluate the information you find."

   Not That: "You can't trust anything online."

3. **Say This:** "Remember, your worth is not determined by likes or comments on social media."

   Not That: "Why do you care so much about likes?"

4. **Say This:** "Screen time can be fun, but it's also important to balance it with outdoor play and other activities." **Not That:** "You're always glued to that screen!"

5. **Say This:** "Let's have open conversations about what you do and see online. I'm here to guide and protect you." **Not That:** "The internet is a dangerous place, you shouldn't be on it."

PART 6 - LIFE SKILLS

Ahh, life skills. The stuff that prepares our teens and young adults for the 'real world'. From managing time, budgeting money, to overcoming the notorious nemesis: procrastination. For many of us, it's a scramble to jam these skills into our children before they fly out of our nests and into the world. And in the mad dash, authoritarian methods such as rigid routines, strict allowances, and severe punishments for procrastination can be tempting. But let's be real, does anyone ever *really* learn from being grounded or having their pocket money slashed?

Instead, gentle parenting allows us to take a different route. It's more of a scenic drive where we foster life skills through guidance, discussions, and modelling. By adopting this approach, we're nurturing self-motivated, resilient, and competent young adults who can navigate life's twists and turns.

Of course, even in the most carefully planned scenic drives, we may end up in a ditch. Maybe it's an overspent allowance, a procrastinated assignment, or a time management disaster. But, remember, we're all human and humans make mistakes. It's not the mistake but the learning from it that matters.

If you've been a drill sergeant before, don't fret! You can start afresh by admitting your past approach wasn't perfect and expressing a desire to change. Involve them in decision-making, discuss different perspectives, and be open to learning from them too. It's never too late to switch from being a control tower to a guidepost.

So, fasten your safety gear and let's embark on this journey of fostering life skills. Believe me, the road may be bumpy but the views, the learning, and the connections are all worth it. The joy of watching your teen blossom into a self-assured adult who can manage life's ups and downs is one of parenting's greatest rewards. So let's get to it!

6.1. Time Management

Time management is crucial in a young adult's life. Here's how to approach it:

1. **Say This:** "I've noticed you seem stressed. Can we look at your schedule together and figure out a plan?"
Not That: "You're always rushing around at the last minute."

2. **Say This:** "It's okay to take breaks. Overworking can lead

to burnout."
Not That: "You're always wasting time."

3. **Say This:** "Prioritizing can help you manage your time better. Let's try it together."
Not That: "Why can't you get your act together?"

4. **Say This:** "Remember, it's okay to say 'no' when you're overwhelmed."
Not That: "You're always overcommitting."

5. **Say This:** "Finding a balance can be tough. Let's navigate this together."
Not That: "You never have time for anything."

6.2. Money Management

Financial literacy is a must. Here's how to guide your young adult:

1. **Say This:** "Let's learn about budgeting together. It's a great tool to manage your expenses."
Not That: "You're always out of money."

2. **Say This:** "Saving up for something you want can be rewarding. Let's try it."
Not That: "You're always asking for more."

3. **Say This:** "Understanding the value of money can help you make wise decisions."
Not That: "You don't know the value of a dollar."

4. **Say This:** "Mistakes are opportunities to learn. Let's figure out what went wrong with your budget this month." **Not That:** "I told you so."

5. **Say This:** "Money doesn't define your worth or success."
Not That: "If only you were more responsible."

6.3. Procrastination

Procrastination can be a big hurdle. Here's how to address it:

1. **Say This:** "Breaking tasks into smaller parts can make them less overwhelming. Would you like some help?"
Not That: "You always wait until the last minute."

2. **Say This:** "It's okay to ask for help if you're feeling stuck."
Not That: "You're just being lazy."

3. **Say This:** "Perfectionism can lead to procrastination. Done is better than perfect."
Not That: "You're always aiming too high."

4. **Say This:** "Focusing on the process rather than the outcome can make tasks more manageable."

Not That: "You're always avoiding work."

5. **Say This:** "Let's find a routine that works for you."
Not That: "Why can't you be more disciplined?"

6.4 Developing Responsibility

Teens and Young Adults need to learn about responsibility, and we can teach them by saying this:

1. **Say This:** "Making your bed every morning can be a great way to start the day off feeling productive."
Not That: "You're so lazy, can't you even make your bed?"

2. **Say This:** "Let's create a weekly cleaning schedule together so we can keep our home tidy."
Not That: "This house would be a mess without me!"

3. **Say This:** "How about we cook dinner together? It's a useful skill and can be a lot of fun."
Not That: "You need to learn to cook, you can't eat takeout forever."

4. **Say This:** "It's your responsibility to manage your homework. Can we set up a system to help you keep track?" **Not That:** "You're so disorganized. Can't you even manage your homework?"

5. **Say This:** "I noticed you've been forgetting to feed the dog. What can we do to help you remember?"
Not That: "If I didn't feed the dog, he'd starve because of your forgetfulness!"

PART 7 - FUTURE PLANNING

Picture this. You're sitting at the dinner table and casually ask your teen about their plans for the future. You're met with the classic eye-roll and a mumbled, "I don't know, okay?" Now what?

In moments like these, it can be tempting to pull out the authoritarian card, dictating the "proper" path they should take, or instilling in them our own unfulfilled ambitions. But, does this approach work? More often than not, it backfires. It can lead to resentment, rebelliousness, and worse yet, your child pursuing a future they're not passionate about.

That's where gentle parenting shines. It involves providing guidance, not mandates. Encouraging exploration, not prescribing the destination. Our role is to open doors, present possibilities, and provide support as they navigate the landscape of their future. This approach fosters confidence, initiative, and most importantly, the courage to follow their own path.

Will this always be smooth sailing? Absolutely not. The terrain of future planning is often a mountainous one, filled with crevices of doubt, steep inclines of pressure, and rocky patches of indecision. But remember, it's okay to slip and slide. It's okay to change paths. What's important is the resilience to keep climbing, keep exploring.

If you've been the 'helicopter parent', hovering over every decision, it's okay to change course. Start by acknowledging your previous approach and express your intention to provide them more autonomy. Provide resources, share experiences, encourage their interests, but ultimately, let them be the captain of their ship.

In this section, we'll explore how to handle the various aspects of future planning gently, fostering an environment that encourages exploration, independence, and confidence. After all, our goal is to raise self-assured adults who can face the future with optimism, preparedness, and zest, not just kids who 'follow the plan.' So, let's GOOO!

7.1. Academic Pressure

Academic pressure can be intense. Here's how to approach it:

1. **Say This:** "Your worth isn't defined by your grades. You're

more than a test score."
Not That: "Why can't you get better grades?"

2. **Say This:** "Learning is more important than grades. Let's focus on understanding the material."
Not That: "Did you study enough?"

3. **Say This:** "It's okay to ask for help when you're struggling with your studies."
Not That: "You should be able to do this on your own."

4. **Say This:** "Finding balance between academics and personal life is crucial. Let's work on that."
Not That: "You're always studying."

5. **Say This:** "Failure is a part of learning. Let's figure out what didn't work and try again."
Not That: "I expected better from you."

7.2. Career Guidance

Career decisions can be overwhelming. Here's how to guide your young adult:

1. **Say This:** "Exploring different career paths can help you find what you truly enjoy."
Not That: "Why don't you choose a 'stable' career?"

2. **Say This:** "Your career should bring you satisfaction, not just financial security."
Not That: "You can't make a living out of that."

3. **Say This:** "It's okay to change your mind about your career choices. It's a journey."
Not That: "You're always indecisive."

4. **Say This:** "Career setbacks are normal. They're part of the journey."
Not That: "I told you it wouldn't work out."

5. **Say This:** "Let's explore different career options together. We'll find the right fit."
Not That: "You should follow in my footsteps."

6. **Say This:** "Choosing a career is about finding what you're passionate about and how you can make a living from it."
Not That: "You can't make a living from painting. Choose a real job."

7. **Say This:** "You might not know what you want to do yet and that's okay. We'll explore options together."
Not That: "You should have figured this out by now."

8. **Say This:** "I know you're worried about your grades, but remember, they don't define your future success."
Not That: "If you don't get good grades, you'll never get a good job."

9. **Say This:** "Let's find out what kind of jobs would align with your interests and skills."
Not That: "Why can't you be more like your cousin who's a doctor?"

10. **Say This:** "It's okay if your career path isn't a straight line. Most people's aren't."
Not That: "You can't keep changing your mind about what you want to do."

PART 8 - RISKY ENCOUNTERS

What's scarier than watching a horror movie alone at midnight? Well, if you're a parent of a teen or young adult, it's probably the thought of your child dabbling in risky behavior.

Before we descend into full panic mode, remember this: risk-taking is a natural part of adolescence and young adulthood. This stage in their life is about pushing boundaries, making mistakes, and learning from them. But as parents, it's instinctive to want to wrap them in a safety bubble, saving them from all harm. The authoritarian method might appear like the quickest fix - set down strict rules and expect full compliance. However, this approach can often lead to rebellion, secrecy, and resentment.

Instead, let's pull up our gentle parenting boots. How does this work? It begins with an open dialogue about potential risks, understanding their point of view, and then setting boundaries together. It's not about painting the world as a big bad wolf waiting to pounce but providing them the tools to make informed decisions. When we approach risk in this way, it empowers them, builds their self-esteem, and strengthens their decision-making abilities.

Does this mean everything will go perfectly? No. We're all human, and sometimes, despite our best intentions, we fumble, and that's okay. It's essential to reassure your teen that no mistake is too big for them to recover, and no mess-up is large enough to jeopardize your love for them.

And if you've been the "rule enforcer" so far, it's never too late to change gears. Start by acknowledging your fears and express your intention to adopt a more open approach. It might be tough, but it's worth it. Because our goal is to foster a relationship where our teens feel comfortable discussing their challenges with us, knowing we are their allies, not just their disciplinarians.

In this section, we'll navigate the sensitive topic of risky encounters and how to maintain open lines of communication, fostering a relationship built on trust and mutual respect. So, let's set sail into this often turbulent, yet immensely crucial aspect of their journey to adulthood.

8.1. Risky Behavior

Here's how to talk about risky behavior:

1. **Say This:** "Making mistakes is part of growing up. Let's talk about what happened."
Not That: "How could you be so irresponsible?"

2. **Say This:** "I care about your safety. Can we discuss how to make safer choices?"
Not That: "You're always getting into trouble."

3. **Say This:** "Understanding consequences can help you make informed decisions."
Not That: "Why can't you think before you act?"

4. **Say This:** "It's okay to say 'no' when you're uncomfortable. Your boundaries matter."
Not That: "Why didn't you stand up for yourself?"

5. **Say This:** "You can always talk to me, no matter what."
Not That: "I can't believe you did that."

8.2. Substance Use and Addiction

Addressing substance use and addiction can be difficult. Here's how to handle it:

1. **Say This:** "I noticed some changes in your behavior and it concerns me. Can we talk about it?"
Not That: "I know you're using drugs/alcohol."

2. **Say This:** "If you're feeling pressured to use substances, we can brainstorm ways to handle these situations."
Not That: "Just say no."

3. **Say This:** "Addiction is a disease, not a failure of character. We can seek help together if you're ready."
Not That: "You're throwing your life away."

4. **Say This:** "Remember, it's okay to ask for help. We're in this together."
Not That: "You're on your own if you choose to continue

using."

5. **Say This:** "Recovery can be a long journey, but I believe in your strength and resilience."

Not That: "Why can't you just stop?"

6. **Say This:** "It's normal to be curious about alcohol and drugs, but they can have serious consequences. Let's discuss them."

Not That: "Only losers do drugs."

7. **Say This:** "If you're ever in a situation where you're uncomfortable, know you can call me, no questions asked." **Not That:** "You better not ever let me catch you drinking."

8. **Say This:** "Remember, just because your friends may be experimenting doesn't mean you have to."

Not That: "You need to stop hanging out with those kids."

9. **Say This:** "Alcohol and drugs can affect your brain development. It's important to make informed decisions."

Not That: "Don't ruin your life with bad choices."

10. **Say This:** "I understand you might feel pressured to try substances, but there are safer ways to fit in."

Not That: "If you try drugs, you're grounded."

PART 9 - UNDERSTANDING THEIR WORLD

Welcome to the final frontier of our guide, folks - a section where we embark on an epic journey to truly comprehend the universe our teens and young adults inhabit. With the advent of an ever-evolving digital culture, nuanced social issues, and the complexity of emotions they navigate daily, understanding their world is crucial - and often as complicated as solving a Rubik's cube blindfolded.

Traditional parenting techniques often focus on control and authority, which may inadvertently create an "us vs. them" scenario. This approach might make teens feel misunderstood and isolated, reducing the chances of them opening up about their world to you. On the flip side, gentle parenting encourages empathy, curiosity, and understanding - it's like exchanging that Rubik's cube for a bridge that links your world with theirs.

By striving to comprehend their world through a lens of empathy and non-judgmental curiosity, you're fostering a relationship that can endure the trials and tribulations of life. The beauty of this approach is that it's an investment with rich returns - a deepened connection that extends beyond these turbulent years, leading to a lifelong relationship based on mutual respect and understanding.

Of course, remember we're only human - sometimes, we'll misstep, misunderstand, and maybe even make a mess. That's okay! It's part of the process. What's more important is our willingness to acknowledge our mistakes and make amends. If you've been 'lost in translation' before, it's never too late to say, "I'm sorry, I misunderstood. Can we start again?"

In this section, we'll take a deep dive into their world, offering you 'say this, not that' strategies to better understand and support your child's unique journey. Ready to wear their shoes and walk a mile or two? Let's step into their world.

9.1 - Social Media Trends

Let's face it, the digital terrain of social media trends can feel like foreign territory, but it's a vital part of your teen's world.

1. **Say This:** "I noticed this new trend on TikTok. Can you explain why it's so popular?"

Not That: "I don't get why you kids are so obsessed with these silly trends."

2. **Say This:** "I'm curious about how you decide which trends to follow."

Not That: "You shouldn't follow trends just because everyone else is."

3. **Say This:** "It's cool how social media lets you explore new ideas and trends. How does this one fit with your interests?"

Not That: "These trends are all so superficial."

4. **Say This:** "You seem to be enjoying this trend. Do you mind sharing what you like about it?"

Not That: "I think it's a waste of time to follow such trends."

5. **Say This:** "Remember, it's perfectly okay to not follow a trend if you don't resonate with it."

Not That: "You need to stop following every trend that comes up."

9.2 - Understanding Modern Slang

Modern slang can seem like a foreign language, but it's an integral part of your child's communication with their peers.

1. **Say This:** "I heard you use the term 'lit'. Can you explain what it means?"

Not That: "Stop using those silly words!"

2. **Say This:** "It's fascinating how language evolves. Could you teach me some of the terms you and your friends use?"

Not That: "Why can't you just speak proper English?"

3. **Say This:** "How do you feel when you use slang? Does it

make you feel more connected to your friends?"
Not That: "Speaking in slang won't get you anywhere in life."

4. **Say This:** "It's important to know when it's appropriate to use slang and when it's not."
Not That: "You sound uneducated when you use slang."

5. **Say This:** "Remember, your words are a reflection of you. Let's explore how to balance using slang with being articulate."
Not That: "You're going to regret talking like this when you're older."

9.3 - Embracing Diversity

In the current global landscape, embracing diversity is more than just a nice-to-have trait, it's essential for their overall personal development and worldview.

1. **Say This:** "We live in a diverse world and it's important to respect all cultures. Let's learn about them together." **Not That:** "Why can't they just adapt to our ways?"

2. **Say This:** "The beauty of our world lies in its diversity. We can learn so much from different cultures."
Not That: "Their traditions are so strange."

3. **Say This:** "People may look, speak, or live differently than us, but we share the same human emotions."
Not That: "They're just so different from us."

4. **Say This:** "Embracing diversity helps us understand and appreciate different perspectives. It's a wonderful thing."

Not That: "I just don't get why they have to do things that way."

5. **Say This:** "Remember, everyone has a unique story. Let's seek to understand and appreciate that."

Not That: "If they want to live here, they should do things our way."

9.4 - Eco-Consciousness

In a world grappling with climate change, fostering an eco-conscious mindset in our young ones is imperative.

1. **Say This:** "It's inspiring to see your generation taking a stand for the environment. How can we make more eco-friendly choices at home?"

Not That: "Don't you think you're taking this climate change thing too far?"

2. **Say This:** "I'd love to hear your thoughts on how we can reduce our carbon footprint."

Not That: "Why bother? One family can't make a difference."

3. **Say This:** "It's wonderful that you're passionate about the environment. Let's learn more about sustainable living together."

Not That: "This eco-friendly trend is just a fad."

4. **Say This:** "Your commitment to protecting the planet is admirable. Let's find more ways to implement it."

Not That: "I think you're getting obsessed with this eco-consciousness thing."

5. **Say This:** "Remember, every little effort counts when it

comes to saving our planet. Your voice matters."
Not That: "Your small actions won't make a difference in the grand scheme of things."

9.5 Listening to Their Worldviews

Our kiddos may harbor ideas that are brand new to us. Be curious about how they see the world.

1. **Say This:** "I respect your beliefs and opinions, even if they differ from mine. Let's talk more about this."

Not That: "You're too young to have a valid opinion."

2. **Say This:** "I see you feel strongly about this. Let's understand your perspective better."

Not That: "You're wrong."

3. **Say This:** "It's great to see you standing up for what you believe in. Let's discuss ways you can make an impact."
Not That: "You can't change the world."

4. **Say This:** "I appreciate your fresh perspective on this matter. It makes me think."

Not That: "You don't know what you're talking about."

5. **Say This:** "We may not always agree, but I value your thoughts. Let's agree to listen to each other."

Not That: "My house, my rules."

PART 10 - EDUCATION

Hello, Parents of the Modern Age! Get ready, because we're about to delve into a topic that's as thrilling as a rollercoaster ride (and at times equally terrifying): The intricacies of navigating our children's education in this rapidly changing world.

Why should we approach this with a gentle parenting touch, you ask? Because the traditionally authoritarian style of "You'll study this because I said so" can backfire, breeding resentment and resistance rather than instilling a love of learning. This hard-nosed approach risks undermining their individual interests and may lead to a lack of motivation. In contrast, gentle parenting validates our children's experiences and respects their individuality, fostering an internal motivation to learn and explore the world around them.

The long-term benefits are numerous! Your child won't just be learning to pass exams; they'll be developing a lifelong love for learning, creativity, and critical thinking skills. By gently guiding them through their education, you're preparing them to navigate life, not just school. And you're strengthening your bond along the way - a priceless advantage in the tumultuous teen years.

Let's remember we're all human here. There will be times when you'll want to pull your hair out in frustration. Maybe you've already had a few such episodes. It's okay. We've all been there. And we'll probably visit again. Some conversations will feel more like negotiations at the United Nations rather than casual chats at the kitchen table. That's fine. No one expects perfection.

Have you ever used the dreaded 'because I said so' line? Have you enforced rigid rules with your child's schooling and homework? It's never too late to change that approach. Kids are more resilient and forgiving than we give them credit for.

Start by acknowledging past mistakes, apologize if necessary, and express your intention to make things better. Encourage their input on how you can best support their educational journey. This will create an atmosphere of mutual respect and understanding, providing fertile ground for future growth.

So, let's go ahead and take the plunge into this deep pool of educational dilemmas. Together, we can swim rather than sink. After all, we're not just raising kids; we're raising the future.

10.1 Tackling the Challenges of School

Whether virtual, home, or traditional, schooling brings a unique set of challenges. It's where our gentle parenting approach can make a difference, teaching kids resilience rather than resistance.

1. **Say This:** "I see you're grappling with this assignment. How about we try a different approach?"
Not That: "Why can't you just get this done?"

2. **Say This:** "Tests can be tough, but they're just a measure of understanding, not self-worth."
Not That: "Another bad grade? What are you doing wrong?"

3. **Say This:** "Your dedication to learning impresses me more than any letter grade."
Not That: "Only an A is acceptable."

4. **Say This:** "School is about broadening your horizons, not just acing tests."
Not That: "Don't lose focus; your grades matter most."

5. **Say This:** "It's alright to falter. It's the stepping stone to mastery."
Not That: "How could you make this mistake again?"

6. **Say This:** "Let's come up with an organization system that helps you keep track of tasks."
Not That: "Your disorganization is a nightmare."

7. **Say This:** "It seems you're having a hard time with your peers. Let's navigate this together."
Not That: "Just steer clear of troublemakers."

8. **Say This:** "Why don't we design a study routine that suits your style?"
Not That: "Stop procrastinating!"

9. **Say This:** "Remember, your teachers are partners in your learning journey. It's okay to reach out to them."
Not That: "You should solve your own problems."

10. **Say This:** "Balancing schoolwork and extracurricular activities is crucial. Let's find your sweet spot."
Not That: "You're wasting too much time on hobbies."

10.2 Homeschooling Your Child

Homeschooling is a high-wire act - balancing educational needs with parental responsibilities. By adopting a gentle parenting approach, we turn this challenging endeavor into an enriching journey.

1. **Say This:** "Your curiosity is a great asset. Let's dive deeper into this subject."
Not That: "This isn't part of the curriculum."

2. **Say This:** "A structured day is essential, but it's also necessary to take time to recharge."

Not That: "We must stick to the schedule, no exceptions."

3. **Say This:** "As a homeschooling parent, I'm learning alongside you. Let's figure things out together."

Not That: "I can't have all the answers."

4. **Say This:** "Let's set up some social activities to balance your study schedule."

Not That: "You're better off without the distractions of friends."

5. **Say This:** "Part of homeschooling is learning to be self-reliant. I'm here for guidance when you need it."

Not That: "I can't spoon-feed you."

6. **Say This:** "I love seeing you take charge of your learning. Let's continue to foster that."

Not That: "You're not serious about your studies."

7. **Say This:** "A change of scenery can enhance learning. How about a field trip?"

Not That: "We can't afford a day off."

8. **Say This:** "It's okay to miss traditional school. Let's talk about what you're feeling."

Not That: "Homeschooling was our decision. Deal with it."

9. **Say This:** "Learning extends beyond textbooks. Let's integrate practical life skills into our routine."

Not That: "Focus on your academics."

10. **Say This:** "We're on this homeschooling journey together. We'll figure things out."

Not That: "You need to respect my rules."

10.3 The Traditional School Experience
The traditional school experience, replete with its highs and lows, lays a robust foundation for lifelong learning. Gentle parenting helps in navigating this journey, fostering resilience and empathy.

1. **Say This:** "I see you're having trouble with your homework. Let's figure out a solution together."

    Not That: "You should've paid more attention in class."

2. **Say This:** "Exams can be stressful. Let's develop some coping strategies."

    Not That: "Just study more and stop complaining."

10.4 Balancing Academics and Social Life

Striking a balance between academics and social life can be like walking a tightrope. With gentle parenting, we can equip our children with the skills to maintain this balance, fostering healthy growth in all aspects of their lives.

1. **Say This:** "Your academic achievements are significant, but they're not everything."
   Not That: "Your grades should be your top priority."

2. **Say This:** "Your social interactions are an important part of your growth."

Not That: "You're spending too much time with friends."

3. **Say This:** "It's okay to take a break from studies to enjoy time with friends."

Not That: "You need to study now, not hang out with friends."

4. **Say This:** "I see you're struggling to juggle schoolwork and social activities. Let's find a solution together."

Not That: "You just need to manage your time better."

5. **Say This:** "Let's set some boundaries to ensure you're getting the most out of your academic and social lives."
Not That: "You need to learn to say no to your friends."

6. **Say This:** "I understand you want to excel in your studies, but it's also important to nurture your relationships."
Not That: "There's no time for friends during exams."

7. **Say This:** "Participation in group activities can help enhance your social skills."

Not That: "You're wasting your time with those club activities."

8. **Say This:** "Let's work out a schedule where you have time for both homework and fun."

Not That: "Fun comes after homework. No negotiations."

9. **Say This:** "I appreciate your dedication to your studies, but remember to enjoy your teenage years."

Not That: "You can have fun after you get into a good college."

10. **Say This:** "It's okay to let loose sometimes. Everyone needs a breather."

Not That: "You can't afford to relax with your grades."

10.5 Addressing Emotional Well-being Amidst School Stress

In the scramble to meet academic demands, mental health often takes a backseat. Through gentle parenting, we can ensure our kids know that their emotional well-being is just as important as their grades.

1. **Say This:** "I see that you're stressed about school. Let's talk about it."

   Not That: "School stress is a part of life. Get used to it."

2. **Say This:** "It's okay to take a mental health day when you need it."

   Not That: "You can't miss school just because you're feeling down."

3. **Say This:** "Let's explore some mindfulness exercises to help manage your stress."

   Not That: "Just relax."

4. **Say This:** "Your feelings are important. It's okay to share them with me."

   Not That: "You're overreacting."

5. **Say This:** "Remember, it's okay to ask for help. If you're feeling overwhelmed, we can find someone to talk to."

   Not That: "You need to handle your problems yourself."

6. **Say This:** "Let's practice some relaxation techniques to help manage your school stress."
Not That: "There's no time for relaxation; you have exams."

7. **Say This:** "Your mental well-being is my priority. Let's find a balance that suits you."
Not That: "You'll feel better once your grades improve."

8. **Say This:** "Expressing your feelings can be therapeutic. It's okay to vent."
Not That: "Stop being dramatic."

9. **Say This:** "It's okay to reach out to a professional for mental health support."
Not That: "You don't need a therapist, you just need to study."

10. **Say This:** "Taking care of your mental health is a sign of strength, not weakness."
Not That: "You're just using stress as an excuse."

10.6 Addressing Resistance and Disinterest in Schoolwork
Resistance and disinterest in schoolwork can be challenging to tackle. Gentle parenting can help us understand the root of these issues, helping children overcome these barriers and reignite their love for learning.

1. **Say This:** "I notice you've been avoiding your schoolwork. Let's talk about what's going on."
Not That: "Stop being lazy."

2. **Say This:** "It's okay to not enjoy every subject equally. Let's find a way to make it more engaging for you."
Not That: "You just need to try harder."

3. **Say This:** "I see you're having a tough time with this assignment. How can I help you?"
Not That: "Just get it done."

4. **Say This:** "Your frustration is valid. Let's take a short break and then try again."
Not That: "You're just giving up too easily."

5. **Say This:** "If you're feeling overwhelmed, we can always ask your teacher for help."
Not That: "You should be able to do this on your own."

6. **Say This:** "It's okay if you're struggling with this assignment. We can figure it out together."
Not That: "You're just not trying hard enough."

7. **Say This:** "If this method isn't working for you, let's find a different way to understand this concept."
Not That: "You have to do it the way it's taught."

8. **Say This:** "It's okay if this subject doesn't excite you as much. Every subject is a building block for your overall development."
Not That: "You have to like this subject to do well."

9. **Say This:** "It's alright to take a break when you're feeling overwhelmed. It can help you come back stronger."
Not That: "Don't waste time taking breaks."

10. **Say This:** "If you're finding it difficult to concentrate, let's try to create a more conducive environment for you." **Not That:** "Your inability to focus is your problem."

A FINAL NOTE ON YOUR EMPOWERED GENTLE PARENTING JOURNEY

Dear Empowered Gentle Parent,

Your road as a parent is winding, thrilling, challenging, and incredibly fulfilling. But it's a journey, not a race.

Through the pages of this book, I've been your Cyrano de Bergerac, whispering the words into your ear. You've been courageous enough to try something strange and new. Most importantly, we've embraced the compassionate method of Gentle Parenting.

These are just tiny pieces of a much bigger puzzle.

We laughed, we learned, and yes, maybe we even shed a tear or two. But we've grown.

The scripts and wisdom in these pages aren't mere words; they're seeds. Seeds that, when nurtured with love, empathy, and consistency, can flourish into the beautiful garden that is your relationship with your teen or young adult.

Let's recall those powerful lessons of body positivity, identity, and consent. Those weren't just chapters; they were conversations, dialogues to engage in with your children, to help them, and YOU, thrive.

But here's the big secret...

It's not a one-and-done deal. It's about trying it on, day by day, moment by moment. And sometimes, it might feel awkward or uncomfortable, like a new pair of shoes. But give it time, wear it in, and see the difference it makes.

Yes, parenting is hard. There will be bumps, and there will be storms. But remember that gentle parenting is like an umbrella; it doesn't stop the rain but helps you walk through it.

So, dear reader, as you close this book, know that you are not closing a chapter in your parenting journey, but opening a door.

A door to empathy. A door to understanding. A door to love.

Embrace it, live it, and know that you are ENOUGH.

Keep shining, keep loving, and most of all, keep being YOU.

Let's Be Loving, Firm, and Fair today,

Lara Pitocchi, M.Ed.
Founder, Empowered Gentle Parenting

P.S. If you're ever in need, please know I'm here for you. We're on this path together, and this book is just the beginning. Flip it open, find what resonates, and let the journey continue. If you are interested in going further, check out the next page.

YOUR NEXT STEPS TO CONTINUE THIS EMPOWERED GENTLE PARENTING JOURNEY

The pages of this book may have ended, but your incredible journey as an Empowered Gentle Parent is just beginning! Use the QR code below to access easy links. Here's how you can continue to grow, connect, and embrace the wonderful world of Gentle Parenting:

1. **Follow Me on Facebook**: Stay up-to-date with all the latest insights, encouragement, and community support. Click that follow button on my Facebook Page and let's stay connected!
2. **Join the Private Empowered Gentle Parenting Facebook Group**: This is where the magic happens! Engage with like-minded parents, share your stories, and let's grow together.
3. **Book a FREE Discovery Call with Me**: Want personalized support and guidance? Schedule a one-on-one discovery call with me, and we'll explore what your unique parenting journey can look like.
4. **Enroll in the 10-Week Empowered Gentle Parenting Program**: Ready to dive deeper? Join this transformative

program designed to give you all the tools, strategies, and support you need to become an Empowered Gentle Parent.
5. **Sign Up for My Newsletter**: Want a regular dose of inspiration, tips, and exclusive content delivered right to your inbox? Sign up for my newsletter and never miss a beat!
6. **Share Your Thoughts**: Loved the book? Have a success story to share? I'd love to hear from you! Share your thoughts, reviews, or even a selfie with the book on social media using the hashtag #EmpoweredGentleParenting.
7. **Spread the Love**: Know a parent who might benefit from this book? Share it with them and spread the love of Gentle Parenting. Together, we can make a difference.

You are not alone on this journey, dear friend. You have a whole community cheering you on, and I'm thrilled to walk this path with you.

Let's be loving, firm and fair today,

Lara Pitocchi, M.Ed. 🤍
Founder, Empowered Gentle Parenting Journey

ABOUT THE AUTHOR

Lara Pitocchi

Lara is an educator and a mom who is passionate about kids. After 25 years in public education, she seeks to help other parents build lifelong connections with their children.

Lara founded Empowered Gentle Parenting to help parents feeling insecure and lost as they break generational trauma cycles and learn to parent mindfully.

Printed in Great Britain
by Amazon